Monotowns

by
Zupagrafika

Photography:
Alexander Veryovkin

ZUPA
GRA
FiKA

Contents

Pretend It's a City: The Fruits of Enlightened Industrialism

What is a monotown? The term would suggest it might be some kind of a city, and this is true in part. The concept relates to towns, but not in the sense of a municipality, rather in relation to a specific set of economical conditions. Some might even say that 'monotown' defines anything but a town.

In 2014 a Russian Federation Government Decree defined when a city can be classified as a monotown. One of the most important factors is the number of people employed in the so-called city-forming factory. If over 20% of the fit-to-work population works in a local industry, the town is listed as a monotown.

A clear definition of these kinds of settlement was necessary for largely social reasons. Cities which rely on the well-being of one single industry tend to be vulnerable to all kinds of economic fluctuations. If the factory isn't doing well, it puts the whole city in danger. And a lot of these factories aren't doing well.

A total of 313 Russian urban settlements were listed as monotowns in 2014. Depending on the state of their economy, the cities were allocated between three groups, which, broadly speaking, consisted of those falling apart, those that were not faring too well and those which seemed OK for the time being. The first category featured 75 monotowns.

Thanks to being included on the list, monotowns might find themselves eligible for state support, preferential economic treatment and the like. Federal aid has had limited success and in 2021 the number of monotowns on the state's list has increased to 321, with a total of 13.5 million inhabitants, who make up more than 9% of the entire population.

In a narrow sense monotowns are the legacy of the Soviet economic system. The Soviet economy was organized according to successive five-year plans, with the whole country operating like an enormous corporation. Monotowns were like different departments within this corporation. Each produced a specific range of products. Bigger cities would produce a variety of goods but many of the smaller ones were built around a single production type – the town of Nikel, for example, is named after its abundance of the eponymous metal ore (nickel), while Mirny is called after the famous 'Mir' kimberlite diamond pipe mine.

As the state controlled both demand and price for every product, there was no risk that market fluctuations could crash the entire economy of those cities. In the context of a planned economy, a city might be perfectly organized around one single factory.

'If the factory isn't doing well, it puts the whole city in danger. And a lot of these factories aren't doing well.'

Another important factor was that the state was able to control its labour resources. It is, undoubtedly, a major undertaking to attract households to live in the city whose economy is built around one industry alone, and even more so if that city is located north of the Arctic Circle, as are Vorkuta or Nikel. In the last 30 years the population of these two cities has shrunk by half.

In a broader sense and from an urban planning perspective, monotowns can be seen as a product of enlightened industrialization. Over the last two centuries there have been numerous attempts at creating the ideal industrial city. It is fascinating to see how all such attempts share a similar format. From above, an industrial city looks like a juxtaposition of separate residential and industrial zones. While the industrial area can differ depending on the type of production, the residential part is pretty much the same everywhere. The living units are designed to be almost identical, often constructed using prefabrication methods, yet with adequate insulation and greenery that seem to compensate for their lack of identity. The multi-storey houses do not line the streets but are instead organized around deep courtyards. There is a programme of public buildings such as kindergartens, schools, and sports facilities scattered around the *microrayons*.

According at least to its own propaganda, the Soviet Union was meant to be the state of the proletariat. It makes sense that enlightened industrialization was its core planning idea. What is more problematic is the way that the entire programme can be seen as a reaction against the industrialization of major European cities in the 19th century. It is this reaction that Friedrich Engels described in his book *The Condition of the*

Working Class in England; and in a way Mirny in Yakutia and other such cities were designed to be the opposite of what Manchester was in the times of Engels.

If the residential areas of *monogorods* all more or less resemble one another, this cannot be said of the factories, of which each is unique. The mines of Norilsk are longer than the Moscow metro. The car industry giant AvtoVAZ in Tolyatti faces the city with a factory shed façade and its check passage is almost 5 km long. The industrial zone of Cherepovets, hometown to the steel giant Severstal, extends over more than 3,000 ha. In what is probably the most beautiful example, the gigantic pit hole that was used to extract diamonds in Mirny forms an integral part of the city`s panorama. In contrast with sealed-off industrial parks, here the overlap between the city and its industry is very much on display. The kimberlite diamond pipe was accessed through surface mining and the result of this effort is clearly visible: a hole in the ground of more than 500 metres in depth and 1,000 metres in width, just a few minutes' walk from the residential area.

So is a monotown a city? From today's perspective the answer is: not exactly. Diversity is key to the contemporary understanding of what makes a city. At least in terms of production, monotowns are the opposite of diverse. They have resulted from efforts to modernize society through industrialization and state control. This model does not, or at least does not seem to, fit the post-industrial economy, although projects like Elon Musk's Gigafactory indicate that industry could one day regain its former pride of place. In its approach to scaling, the Gigafactory looks very much like the industrial zone of Tolyatti.

The Federal government does not seem to have had much success in transforming monotown economies. Perhaps their approach was the wrong way to go. Perhaps what industrial cities need is more industry rather than diversification. Contemporary production can be quite impressive. Melting tonnes of metal in a fully automated giant factory seems way cooler than a laptop job. I had the chance to meet several monotown officials who, like one of the mayors in the Ural region, were sceptical about the concept of economic diversification and did not accept the idea that cities should be independent from the factories that had formed them. In his words, a factory was the best thing that could ever happen to a city. He concluded by stating: 'We want more of it'.

Konstantin Budarin
Independent writer and researcher based in Moscow

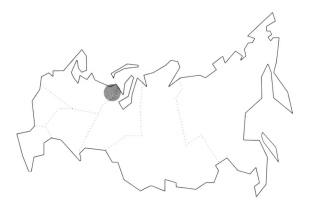

Vorkuta

The locals say that once you arrive in Vorkuta, you become hostage to the Arctic forever. Indeed, there is something about the city that makes you feel caught up within its centre. The city layout forms a closed circuit of 16 settlements, erected out of prefabricated panels around coal mines; this is known as the Vorkuta Ring. The mining infrastructure began to be constructed on the subarctic tundra in the early 1930s by prisoners of the Vorkutlag Gulag. They would be forced to work outside in temperatures falling to -40° Celsius; thus, the labour camp is remembered as the deadliest in European Russia. By the 1950s, Vorkuta had become one of the fastest growing and wealthiest towns in the USSR and its coal supply played a key role during World War II. The high salaries offered by its founding company, Severstal, attracted so many inward migrants that in the 1980s the city's population grew to over 115,000, and new satellite urban areas together with their respective mines popped up further and further into the hinterland. However, from the 1990s onwards, in the face of the harsh climate, long polar nights and limited employment possibilities, population outflow from this area has been alarming. Some of the oldest districts, such as Vorgashor, Yurshor or the buildings on the Shakhtorskaya embankment are now either abandoned or demolished. Those who have not been able to leave unassisted are enrolled on a state resettlement list, but the waiting time for getting assigned a better place in the Russian 'mainland' is so long that it looks unrealistic that elders can hope ever to leave. In order to control the city's depopulation and the houses abandoned in the process, often with all their former tenants' furniture and personal effects left behind in them, the local authorities decided to gradually relocate the residents of the shrinking settlements to renovated vacant apartments in Vorkuta city centre and other neighbouring settlements.

◁◁

Severny settlement, established
in the early 1940s around the
Oktyabrsky mine

△

Bus stop at the Vorkuta
Ring, direction Zapolyarny
settlement

▷

Uninhabited frozen
panel block in
Vorgashor settlement

Large Panel I-335 series block in ul. Engelsa | Built: 1962

Soviet-era mosaic celebrating Bulgarian-Russian friendship on the side elevation of the traffic police department
building in ul. Dimitrova | Built: 1986

Komsomolsky settlement near Vorkuta Ring; set up in 1949,
the urban area is to be closed down with its remaining
population resettled to neighbouring Vorgashor

△

Abandoned flat in
Vorgashor settlement,
established in 1964

Collapsed wooden house in Komsomolsky settlement | Built: 1950s

Polar Quarter in ul. Sedova | Komsomolsky settlement

Five-storey precast panel block | Built: 1986 | Komsomolsky settlement

△

Entrance to Zapolyarny
settlement

▷

'Have a nice trip!' on the way to
Vorkuta airport | ul. Aviatsionnaya

City Archive of Vorkuta in ul. Lenina. Series TPO153-1

Abandoned shop in Yubileyny Pereulok | Vorgashor settlement

'Coal' monument in Vorgashor's central square celebrating the main mineral extracted by the Vorgashorskaya
coal mine | Built: 1985

Lenin monument in ul. Leninskogo Komsomola | Vorgashor settlement

'Glory to the conquerors of the
Arctic' nine-storey residential
building in ul. Dimitrova, also called
the 'Chinese Wall'. Series TP-85
Built: 1981

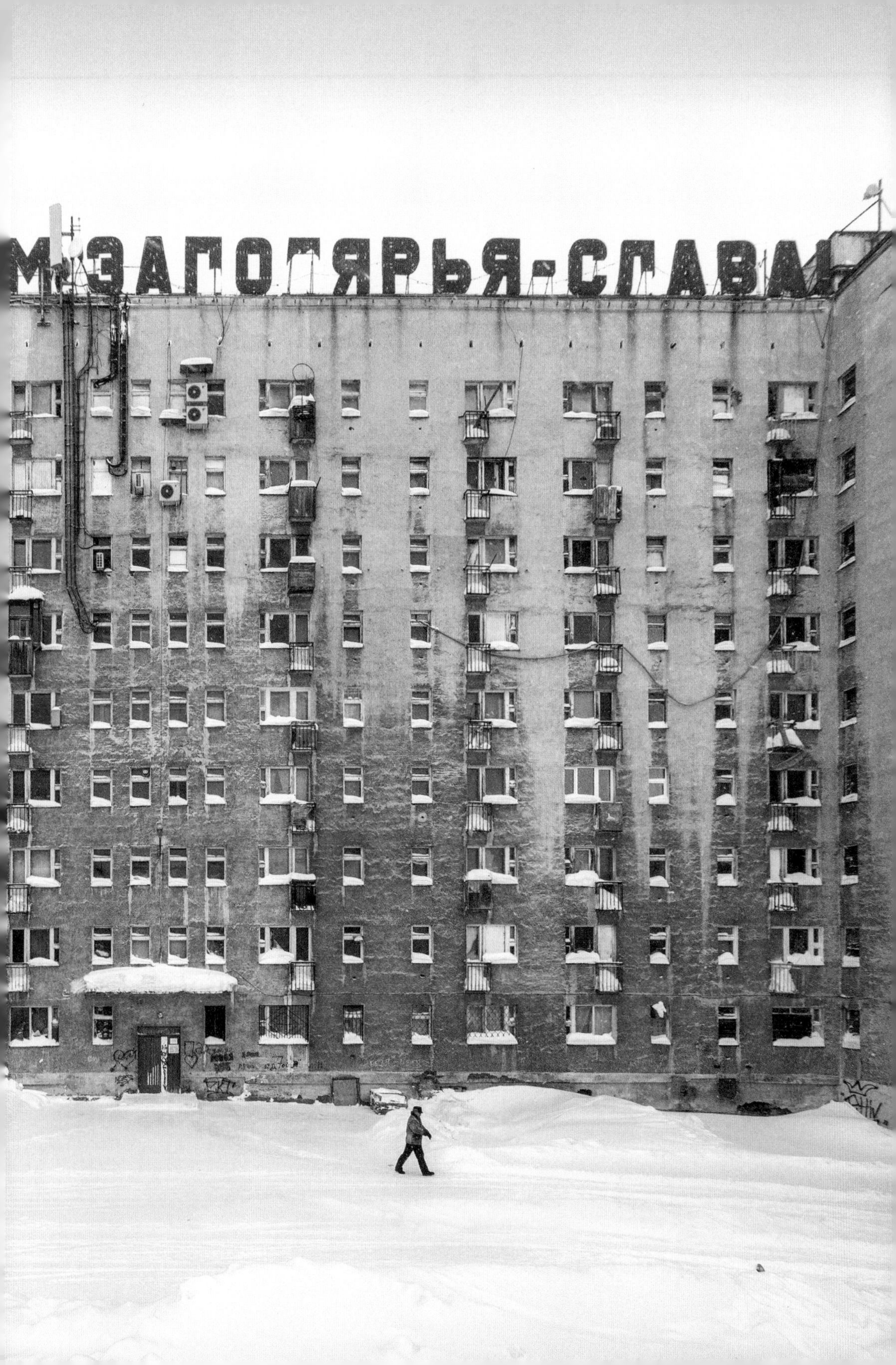
ЗАПОГЯРЬЯ-СЛАВА

Abandoned prefab panel block in ul. Zemlyachki | Zapolyarny settlement

Former 'Ukraine' restaurant, now the House of Culture in ul. Frunze | Zapolyarny settlement

1-335 AY series panel blocks in ul. Timanskaya | Built: 1988 | Timan Microrayon

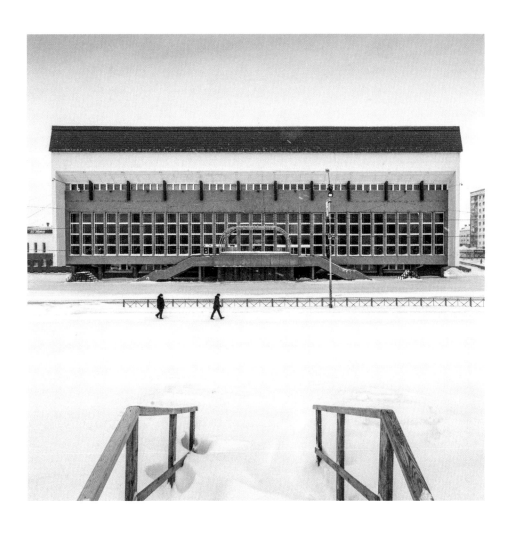

△

Universal sports and visual complex
'Olymp' in ul. Gagarina.
Architect: V.V Martsinkevich.
Built: 1984-1990

▷▷

Abandoned settlement of Yurshor established in
1944 around mine nº 29; officially closed down in the
early 2000s, the ghost town is home to the memorial
cemetery where the prisoners of OLP Gulag are buried

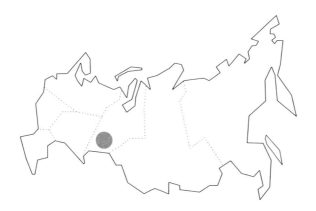

Magnitogorsk

Bordering Kazakhstan and stretching between two continents, Europe and Asia, the Chelyabinsk region became a perfect playground for Stalin's vision of the new industrial Soviet Union in the 1930s. Magnitogorsk was set up at the foot of the 'Magnetic Mountain', a geographical feature so abundant in iron, it is believed to disorientate both compasses and birds flying over it. 'We are becoming a country of metal' said Stalin in 1929 upon implementing the five-year plan to transform the mostly agricultural landscape of the USSR into urban centres surrounding gigantic factories, intended to elevate the Russian economy to the next level. Magnitogorsk Iron and Steel Works, aka 'Magnitka', in the Southern Urals, was erected at lightning speed under huge pressure from Moscow and with consequences of extreme exhaustion, hunger and numerous human fatalities. The empty land around was to become the foundation for the first city on Earth to be planned from scratch. However, the functional linear city commissioned from German architect Ernst May has never fully materialized and the only trace of his urban plan are several rows of small brick houses erected next to the plant which form an industrial estate called Sotsgorod ('Socialist City'). Mass urban development based on serialization and prefabrication was only realized after WWII, when a bridge connection was built across the Factory Pond, separating not only Magnitogorsk's industrial left bank from its residential right bank, but also the continent of Europe from that of Asia. But the monotown is not only famous for its unusual geographic location. 'During the Great Patriotic War, every second tank and every third shell was made of Magnitogorsk steel', says the inscription in Victory Square and proudly towering above the city since 1979, the impressive 15-metre high monument *Rear-Front* shows a steel worker handing a sword to a soldier, commemorating those merits.

◁◁ | △

Lenin monument in front of the MMK
(Magnitogorsk Iron and Steel Works)
Komsomolskaya Ploshchad
Leninsky District

▷

13-storey tower block in ul. Truda
Series 14-5175-AS | Built: 1990
Microrayon 142
Ordzhonikidzevsky District

Agapovka, a village east of Magnitogorsk where the flux limestone deposits used by the 'Magnitka' plant were discovered

View of the Microrayon 134 prefab panel blocks | Ordzhonikidzevsky District

Industrial zone in ul. Lugovaya | Leninsky District

△

▷▷

Magnitogorsk State Circus in ul.
Gryaznova | Architects: L. B. Segal,
E.S. Akopov, I.A. Shadrin
Built: 1976 Pravoberezhny District

pp. 48-49: Housing estate
along ul. Zeleny Log,
as seen from ul. Zhukova
Ordzhonikidzevsky District

Nine-storey tower block in ul. Tevosyana | Built: 1990s | Microrayon 143
Ordzhonikidzevsky District

△

86 series housing unit
in ul. Gryaznova
Built: early 1990s
Pravoberezhny District

▷

'Tyl Frontu' monument of an MMK steel
worker and a soldier commemorating
the Great Patriotic War | Sculptor: L.N.
Golovnitsky | Built: 1979

Nine-storey residential complex in ul. Voznesenskaya | Pravoberezhny District

Boiler room pipe, as seen from ul. Truda and Prospekt Lenina | Microrayon 136 | Ordzhonikidzevsky District

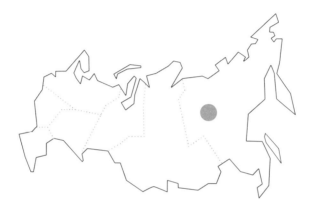

Mirny

The monotown of Mirny lies on the verge of a 525m deep and 1,200m wide pit hole, into which its urban tissue appears to be on the point of falling at any minute. In fact, the entire micro-universe of Mirny seems to revolve around one of the largest human-made excavations on Earth, visible even from space. The history of the city dates back to 1955 when kimberlite diamond deposits were accidentally discovered during a geological expedition to Yakutia, now Sakha Republic, part of the Russian Federal District of the Far East. At the end of the 1950s, the state diamond enterprise NPO Yakutalmaz erected the first wooden houses, *BAMovskiye doma*, and other facilities for the mine workers and their families. Similarly to the city of Norilsk, everything needed to be constructed on concrete piles that protect the permafrost from the heat emitted by the buildings. Thanks to the special research institute Yakutniproalmaz whose task was to come up with urban solutions to the extreme temperatures – which fall to -35° Celsius in the winter – today there are almost no five-storey *khrushchyovka* blocks in Mirny. Instead, solid nine-storey blocks with 70 cm-thick external panel walls and good thermal insulation characterize the northern housing estate of the Soviet era. Although diamonds are said to be 'forever', there are serious doubts whether they may truly be so for the city of Mirny. With the collapse of the USSR in 1992, the Mirny mine was taken over by a private company which has continued to extract kimberlite here. However, the mine's reserves have been receding considerably year by year and all mining has had to be moved underground. Moreover, following the tragic flood that trapped over 100 employees underground in 2017, the pit underwent a temporary closure. According to specialists, the mine's natural resources will be exhausted within 20-30 years from now, putting into question this single-industry city's future.

◁◁ | △ The Mirny pit shaft, 525m deep and 1,200m wide, is visible from space; the largest diamond mined here was named '26th Congress of the Communist Party of the Soviet Union'

Passage under the residential building erected on concrete piles, ul. Lenina

Nine-storey precast panel
estate in ul. Soldatova
Built: early 1990s

Entrance to Mirny City

Dredge 201, part of ALROSA's diamond dredging fleet on the Irelyakh River, lifting diamond-bearing sands from the river bottom

◁◁

View of Mirny monotown from the Mir diamond mine. Open-cast
mining began here in 1957 and was moved underground in 2009

△

Soviet-era mosaic in front
of Mirny airport

Carousel in Gorodskoy Park: 'Mo Gorod Mirny'

'Mir Diamond Pipe Discoverers' monument | Authors: E. Ermolaev, E. Temnikov, Y. Kafengauz
Built: 1970

◁◁

Wooden houses and nine-
storey prefab panel block
in ul. 40 let Oktyabrya

△

The 'Serp i Molot' ('Hammer
and Sickle') sculpture in
Leningradsky Prospekt

▷▷

Pp. 76-77: Rudovoznaya
Doroga around 'Mir'
kimberlite diamond mine

'Aibolit and Animals' sculpture in front of the Central Polyclinic

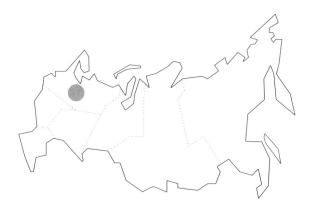

Cherepovets

While most former monotowns in Russia were established during the Soviet era as extensions of local industries, Cherepovets originates in the 14th century when the village of Fedosyevo was founded in today's Vologda Oblast on the Sheksna River. But it was not until 1947 that the construction of Severstal, the largest metallurgical plant in Russia, caused the city to re-emerge as a sizable, 300,000-inhabitant, urban centre where industrial growth went hand in hand with the robust development of the sports and cultural sectors. With its generous offer of museums and monuments, by the 1990s Cherepovets earned itself the nickname of the 'The Athens of the North'. In 2012 another big manufacturer specializing in phosphate-based fertilizers built its infrastructure in the northern district of Severny. However, despite offering an alternative and attractive employment opportunity in the area, JSC Apatit also brought the city notoriety, adding to a level of air pollution unparalleled by any other city in the world, excluding Norilsk. Thanks to frequent northerly winds, the exhaust fumes from both the Industrialny and Severny districts travel over the Yagorba River to the left bank Zayagorbsky District, which is home to over one third of the city's population, who inhabit omnipresent concrete *panelki* stretching as far as the eye can see. The residential area, locally known as 'Zarechye', did not ultimately furnish city dwellers with the desired seclusion from the harmful industrial waste emitted on the right bank, as had originally been planned. High hopes are now held for the southern district, Zasheksninsky, known as Prostokvashino, and connected to the city by the 780 metre-long impressive Oktyabrsky Bridge, whose former villages, including Maturino and Gritino, have been transformed into Cherepovets's new 'sleeping district'.

Residential tower blocks and the Yagorbsky Bridge, as seen from the Sheksna River embankment
Industrialny District

◁◁

Palace of Metallurgists,
ul. Stalevarov
Built: late 1970s - 1993
Industrialny District

△

Secondary school nº 2
Built: late 1970s
Microrayon 25
Zayagorbsky District

▷

Cherepovets Metallurgical
Plant PJSC Severstal
Severnoye Shosse
Industrialny District

125-048 / 1.2 series prefab panel block in ul. Krasnodontsev | Built: 1989 | Zayagorbsky District (Zarechye)

Side facade detail of a *panelka* in ul. Arkhangelskaya. Series 1-467 | Built: 1977 | Microrayon 21

Zayagorbsky District (Zarechye)

View of the Yagorba River
embankment | Microrayon 9

'Teploenergo' Boiler House n° 2 in Microrayon 25 | Built: 1983 | Zayagorbsky District (Zarechye)

△

Oktyabrsky Bridge across Sheksna River
linking Zasheksninsky with Industrialny
District | Built: 1979

▷▷

Fishermen on the Sheksna River with the
Cherepovets Metallurgical Plant in the
background

Prefab panel housing complex in ul. Ostinskaya | Built: 1999 | Microrayon 219 | Severny District

Panelki estate in ul. Ostinskaya | Microrayon 218 | Severny District

◁◁

Nine-storey housing complex in ul. Krasnodontsev
Built: 1989 | Microrayon 25 | Zayagorbsky
District (Zarechye)

△

Brick residential complex
in Microrayon 229
Severny District

Housing estate in ul. Khimikov | Microrayon 20 | Zayagorbsky District (Zarechye)

Five-storey housing unit in ul. Molodezhnaya | Microrayon 221 | Severny District

Residential complex in ul. Partizan Okinina | Built: 1990 | Microrayon 222 | Severny District

16-storey high-rise tower block in ul. Danilova | Built: 1990 | Industrialny District

△

Prefab panel in ul. Ostinskaya
Microrayon 219 | Severny District

▷▷

Kolkhoz Market in ul. Maksima Gorkogo
Built: 1976 | Industrialny District

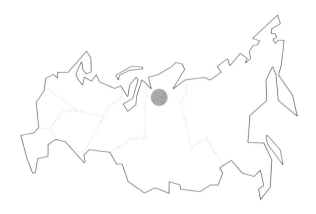

Norilsk

Within rows of concrete panel houses, built as if to defend a medieval fortress from an external enemy, lies the subarctic city of Norilsk. Divided only by narrow passages that allow inhabitants access to their homes, the housing units were laid out in this way to protect the inner city from the biting winds. Their bright pink, green and blue colours contrast with the omnipresent whiteness, helping children to identify their homes during the long polar nights.

Since the 1930s, the history of this northernmost industrial centre has been one of unprecedented human efforts to tame the wild natural environment. It was the Gulag prisoners who were first brought here to build the mining facilities of the city-forming enterprise, Norilsk Nickel, the world's largest extractor of nickel, palladium and platinum. When Norillag closed in 1957, a local 'house factory' started to mass-produce prefabricated panels for a five-storey *khrushchyovka*, providing locals with the city's first decent, climate-proof housing. For almost a century now, the biggest challenge for all construction here has been the perennially-frozen ground. Although by the end of the 20th century it seemed as if the concrete foundation piles that supported all buildings had conquered the permafrost, proving to efficiently protect it from melting, progressive global warming and occasional, negligent urban practices have been leading to more and more ice-sediment thaw which has resulted in many constructions literally falling apart. In addition, melting permafrost is believed to be the cause of some of the most alarming ecological disasters in Arctic history, such as the fuel depot collapse at a power station near Norilsk in 2020, which led to a gigantic spill of diesel oil into the rivers and lakes of the local tundra.

◁◁

Unfinished prefab panel blocks in
Oganer Microrayon | Abandoned
since the mid-1990s

△

Abandoned 84 KOPE-N
housing unit | Built: 1990s
Oganer Microrayon

Entering Norilsk from the west; the 'horns' sign on the road towards the airport

Housing units in ul. Yugoslavskaya | Built: 1993 | Oganer Microrayon

Nine-storey apartment block in ul. Khantayskaya. Series 84 | Built: 1981 | Microrayon 4

Prefab panel housing complex in ul. Ozyornaya | Built: late 1980s | Oganer Microrayon

111-84 series residential building in ul. Komsomolskaya | Built: late 1980s

◁◁

84 series panel block in
ul. Kirova | Built: 1983
Microrayon 15

△

Nine-storey residential building in
Ploshchad Metallurgov | Built: 1984
Microrayon 2-3

CHP - 1 (TETs) combined heat and power plant n° 1 in ul. Talnakhskaya | Built: 1942

△

South entrance to Norilsk
Built: 1950s
Oktyabrskaya Ploshchad

▷▷
Pp. 122-123:
TETs-1 power plant, as seen from
ul. Energeticheskaya

111-112 series panel block in ul. Valkovskaya | Built: late 1980s | Oganer Microrayon

Panelka in ul. Khantayskaya | Built: 1991 | Microrayon 4

△

An-26 aircraft in front of the Nadezhda
Metallurgical Plant named after B. I. Kolesnikov
(Kombinat 'Nadezhda') | Built: 1979

▷▷

View of the colourful prefab panel
houses in Microrayon 2-3, erected
between the 1970s and 1980s

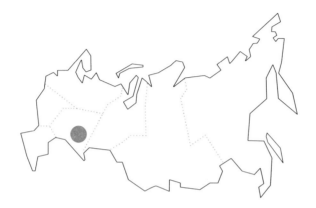

Tolyatti

Tolyatti grew up around the automobile industry as a Soviet city built on an American dream. In the 1960s the Detroit of the East, named for the Italian Communist Party Secretary Palmiro Togliatti, began to slowly materialize on the banks of the Volga River in partnership with the Italian car manufacturer Fiat. The Volzhsky Avtomobilny Zavod, today AvtoVAZ, was to manufacture affordable vehicles for average Soviet families. Their flagship Lada marque quickly flooded the streets of the entire Eastern Bloc and became the most loved and loathed car in the USSR. In succeeding decades, the city expanded proportionately with car production and Tolyatti soon became the largest monotown in Russia. The streets of the new district Avtozavodsky, with residences erected from prefabricated panels especially to house the factory's employees, are exceptionally wide both for driving comfort and to allow winds from the river to sweep away factory exhaust fumes and keep air pollution at bay. The new city is also home to more sophisticated architectural edifices made of steel and concrete, such as the Volgar Sports Palace designed by Yuri Ivanovich Karpukhin in 1968. For the Tolyatti car factory, as for many other state-owned plants, the fall of the Soviet Union equalled privatization. For the inhabitants it meant the end of the city-forming company's public provision in all fields, including good salaries, urban investments, infrastructure, education and health care. They were now left to their own devices and had to survive in the new reality which turned out to be especially brutal when in the mid-1990s both the car production and streets of Tolyatti were taken over by criminal organizations. The monotown's rise and fall has also been almost parallel to that of Detroit, whose success, built on the vision of Henry Ford, came to a spectacular end in 2013. Although Tolyatti also had a close shave, the car plant was eventually rescued from bankruptcy in 2009 by the Russian government and since 2016 it has been part of the French Renault group and has continued to provide employment to the local population.

Shluzovoy Microrayon near Zhigulevskoe More railway station | Built: 1989 | Komsomolsky District

The Scientific and Technical Center of the Volga Automotive Plant | Architect: M. Demidovtsev
Built: late 1980's | Avtozavodsky District

◁◁

The Volgar Sports Palace
Primorskiy Bulvar
Architect: Y. I. Karpukhin
Built: 1969-1975

△

16-storey prefab panel block
in Lunacharsky Bulvar
Built: 1980
Avtozavodsky District

11-60-01 / 16-16T series prefab panel blocks in Shlyuzovoy Microrayon | Built: 1989 | Komsomolsky District

Tile-clad housing unit in ul. Ofitserskaya | Avtozavodsky District

'Matryoshka' residential complex in Moskovsky Prospekt | Avtozavodsky District

◁◁

'DKIT' Culture, Art, and Creativity Palace.
Architect: S. M. Vinograd | Built: 1988
Avtozavodsky District

△

The world's only diesel-electric submarine B-307, in
the K.G. Sakharov Museum (open-air technical and
engineering museum) | Avtozavodsky District

The Automobile Plant District constructed for the AvtoVAZ employees in 1972, as seen from Primorskiy Bulvar

◁◁

High-rise *panelki* in
ul. Zheleznodorozhnaya
Zhigulevskoe More settlement
Komsomolsky District

△

Soviet mosaic and bas-reliefs inside
the 'Olymp' swimming pool, designed
by TsNIIEP (Central Research
Institute for Experimental Design)

Universal sports complex 'Olymp' | Architects: B. Averintsev, I. Bessonova | Built: 1985 | Avtozavodsky District

Tolyatti Thermal Power Station (TETs) in Tsentralny District

AvtoVAZ office building, as seen from K.G. Sakharov museum | Avtozavodsky District

△

Palace of Culture 'Togliatti' (former DK
'Sintezkauchuk') with the 'Prometheus'
titanium decorative panel | Architect: S. M.
Vinograd | Built: 1976

▷▷

Pp. 150-151: Former 'Saturn' cinema
Architects: V.V. Lazarev, I.V. Semeikin, E.B.
Ter-Stepanov, M.P. Bubnov, V.G. Nemirovsky
Operating from 1972 to 2012

'Medgorodok' City Clinical Hospital nº 5 | Architects: V. Adamovich, E. Pekarsky, E. Litvak, O. Emelyanova
Built: 1980s | Avtozavodsky District

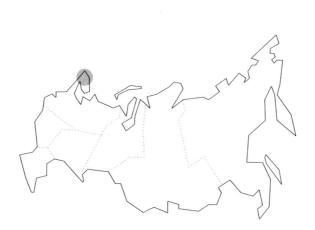

Nikel

December 2020 marked a truly historical moment not only for the population of the Russian Kola Peninsula, but equally for the Norwegian Sør-Varanger region. After over 70 years of emitting alarming quantities of toxic sulphur dioxide into the environment, the Kola Mining and Metallurgical Company (Kola MMC) closed down for good, leaving behind a lifeless lunar landscape of brown burnt-out taiga soils. The picturesque area on lake Kuets'yarvi where the Nornickel plant was built has been a bone of contention between Russia, Norway and Finland for centuries. The first smelter was built in what was then called Nikkeli in 1942 when the city together with the entire Petsamo region belonged to Finland. However, by the time the smelter came into operation, the area had been taken over by the Red Army; it was eventually incorporated back to the USSR in 1944. It was only two years later, when the Soviets started exploring the bountiful local nickel deposits on a mass scale, that Petsamo was renamed Pechengsky District, and Kola MMC became one of the largest palladium and nickel producers worldwide. Most of the prefab panel houses here were constructed in the 1950s, extending the plant south along the main Gvardeyskiy Avenue; it then expanded further west. By the end of the 1980s Nikel marked its peak population rate of over 21,000 inhabitants. However, after it became certain that the mine was closing for good, over 70% of the plant's employees decided to sell their flats and desert the town in a flash. As *the Barents Observer* reported, at the beginning of 2020: 'You can now buy an apartment in Nikel for the price of an iPhone'. Today both the local government and Nornickel are focused on rebuilding Nikel's economy based on appreciation rather than exploitation of its natural environment, in an attempt to make the contaminated Pechenga region green again.

Entry to Nikel from Gvardeyskiy Prospekt

Lenin Monument in front of the Palace of Culture 'Voskhod' in Ploshchad Lenina | Built: 1964

Nine-storey *panelka* in Gvardeyskiy Prospekt | Built: 1989

Transmission towers at the Pechenganickel Mining and Metallurgical Combine

△

Prefab panel housing unit in Gvardeyskiy Prospekt
Series 93 M, 1-464 DN | Built: 1989

▷

Zarechye Microrayon, as seen
from ul. Sovetskaya

◁◁

Pechenganickel plant, part of the Kola Mining and Metallurgical Company Operating between 1946 and 2020

△

The 'Wall of Memory' in Gvardeyskiy Prospekt, commemorating the Great Patriotic War

One of the first houses erected for the Kola MMC smelter employees in the 1950s, currently abandoned

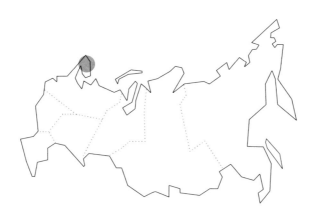

Monchegorsk

'Monche' means beautiful in the Akkala Sami language used by
the indigenous Sami community who inhabit the Kola Peninsula.
But the crystal blue Imandra and Lumbolka lakes, and the Monche-
Tundra mountain range surrounding the city can be very misleading.
Waking up in Monchegorsk might feel like the start of a foggy day
in London, only here the fog is a dense cloud of pollution. The area
is home to nickel cobalt and copper processing factories, as well
as refining and metallurgical workshops, emitting extremely toxic
sulphur dioxide fumes and contaminating the local atmosphere,
soils and waters. The infamous Severonikel (today the JSC Kola
Mining and Metallurgical Company) plant was erected in the early
1930s, with about 20 provisional settlements gradually growing
up around it. In 1937 the metallurgical business skyrocketed
and the small-scale urbanization began to be transformed into
Monchegorsk as we know it today. The urban plan for the city was
commissioned from the Leningrad *Gorstroyproekt*, under the lead
of Sergey Brovtsev, with the aim of transforming the temporary
wooden hut settlements into an actual city representing the might
of the Arctic. The 1950s brought the mass housing construction
boom and following the pattern established in other urban
centres of the former USSR, the monocity was filled with identical
47-series *khrushchyovka* blocks. The town planners learned
from the mistakes of neighbouring Kirovsk and reserved a huge
area of Tsentralny Park for forest plantations in the heart of the
inner-city area. The city's tourism website exhorts: 'Acknowledge
Monchegorsk not as the hell of Kola Peninsula'. Thus, 'the green
lungs' of Monchegorsk can be seen as an especially precious
asset now that the city's policy is oriented towards decreasing air
pollution and becoming more environmentally friendly.

Khrushchyovka in Prospekt Kirova. Series 1-464A-15 | Built: 1976

Ul. Komarova bus stop near the inner-city Komsomolskoye Lake

93-M type panel blocks
in ul. Gruzovaya
Moncha Microrayon

△

Monchegorsk City Council in the main square
Ploshchad Revolyutsii | Architects: V.D.
Chernopyatov, S.S. Bukatov | Built: 1970

Abandoned dormitory 'Chaika' in ul. 10-Y Gvardeyskoy Divizii | Built: 1985

Monchegorsk old town, Imandra and Lumbolka Lakes, and the Cathedral of the Ascension of the Lord, as seen from the top of Poazuaivench Mountain

'The Conquerors of the Monche-Tundra' monument initially located in Ploshchad Revolyutsii, currently in Prospekt Metallurgov | Built: 1967

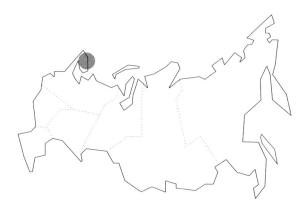

Kirovsk

Picturesque lakes, rivers, tundra and taiga forests and the impressive Khibiny mountains: the natural landscapes of this quaint town above the Arctic Circle could well be mistaken for any tourist resort in the Alps. Indeed, the potential of Kirovsk's scenery has been put to good use by the film industry since the early 20th century, not only in Russian cinema, as in the Oscar-nominated *Leviathan*, but also by American filmmakers. The town's economy, however, does not depend on motion pictures but rather on large deposits of apatite, an ore used to produce fertilizer, first discovered in the nearby settlement of Kukisvumchorr in 1926. Since the 1920s the mine has been owned by one of the biggest agricultural fertilizer producers in the world – Apatit, today part of PhosAgro. By the 1950s Kirovsk had developed into a fully-fledged urban centre populated by migrants brought to the Arctic either by force, or monetary incentives. The numerous state-owned mining industries brought to the Murmansk Region under Stalin flourished on the frozen soils of the Far North, exceptionally bountiful in minerals. The golden era of industries based on extraction, however, came to an end with the fall of the Soviet Union. For Kirovsk, as with other monotowns, this meant teetering on the verge of economic disaster. But thanks to its landscapes, the modernization of its Big Wood Ski Resort and other investment in tourism infrastructure, Kirovsk managed to a great extent to diversify its economy. Today it welcomes increasing numbers of skiers from Russia and Scandinavia; while The Khibiny National Park established in 2018 has opened a new chapter for Kirovsk's image. It seems like the environmentally friendly path the monocity has been paving for itself through recent years is slowly but steadily paying off.

Five-storey *panelka* in Kukisvumchorr Microrayon (also called 'the 25th km')

Prefab panel housing unit in ul. 50 Let Oktyabrya. Series 1-464A

◁◁
Kirovsk Olimpiyskaya estate and Lake
Bolshoy Vudyavr, as seen from the
Bolshoy Vudyavr ski complex

△
Kirovskiy Rudnik Kf Ao Apatit, the oldest
mine in the Khibiny massif, located in
Kukisvumchorr Microrayon

Five-storey housing estate next to the Big Wood ski lift in ul. Olimpiyskaya. Series 111-93 | Built: 1982

Ruins of the Gornyak Palace of
Culture, burned down in the late
1990s | Kukisvumchorr Microrayon
Built: 1934

Central City Library in Prospekt Lenina | Built: 1939

Abandoned Kirovsk-Murmansky railway station, once a symbol of the city's prosperity – in operation from 1939 to 1996

93-011 series prefab panel block in ul. Olimpiyskaya | Built: 1978

Memorial to the residents of Kirovsk who
died in the Great Patriotic War

93-011 series prefab panel block in Verkhnyaya
Doroga, built in 1983, and Kukisvumchorr Mountain

Acknowledgements

Zupagrafika would like to thank Alexander Veryovkin, Konstantin Budarin, Maciej Kabsch, Marta & Maciej Mach, Paquita & Pepe, Kasia & Paweł, Andrés & Judit, Rita & Simón, for their help and support.

Alexander Veryovkin would like to thank Anastasia Makarenko and Maria Samsonova for their support during the shooting.

Authors

Zupagrafika are David Navarro and Martyna Sobecka, an independent publisher, author and graphic design studio, established in 2012 in Poznań, Poland, celebrating modernist architecture, design and photography in a unique and playful way.

Over the last decade, David and Martyna have created, illustrated and published award-winning books exploring the post-war modernist and brutalist architecture of the former Eastern Bloc and beyond, such as *Miasto Blok-How* (2012), *Blok Wschodni* (2014), *Blokowice* (2016), *Brutal London* (Prestel, 2016), *Brutal East* (2017), *The Constructivist* (2017), *Modern East* (2017), *Brutal Britain* (2018), *Hidden Cities* (2018), *Panelki* (2019), *Eastern Blocks* (2019), *Concrete Siberia* (2020), *Brutal Poland* (2020).

Monotowns is a follow-up to *Concrete Siberia* and *Eastern Blocks*. On this occasion, Zupagrafika asked the Russian photographer Alexander Veryovkin to capture the post-war architecture and industrial landscapes around the monotowns of Cherepovets, Kirovsk, Kovdor, Magnitogorsk, Mirny, Monchegorsk, Nikel, Norilsk, Tolyatti and Vorkuta.

Alexander Veryovkin is a photographer, born in 1987 in Leningrad (in the former USSR), currently living and working in St. Petersburg, Russia. He graduated from the Faculty of Mathematics and Mechanics at St. Petersburg State University, majoring in astronomy. His work has been exhibited in museums and art centres in various cities including Amsterdam, Minsk, St. Petersburg and Moscow. He is also the photographer of *Concrete Siberia* (Zupagrafika, 2020). The pictures featured in *Monotowns* were taken over a two-year period during winter, with temperatures reaching -35° Celsius in some locations.

Cover image: Moncha Microrayon (Monchegorsk)
Index image: Oganer Microrayon (Norilsk)
Foreword image: Kovdor Mining and Processing Plant

Published by Zupagrafika
Poznań, Poland. 2021

Printed in Poland
Paper from responsible sources
ISBN 978-83-950574-8-9
www.zupagrafika.com